REMARKABLE

PEOPLE

Queen Rania Al-Abdullah

by Leia Tait

Published by Weigl Publishers Inc.
350 5th Avenue, Suite 3304, PMB 6G
New York, NY 10118-0069

Website: www.weigl.com

Library of Congress Cataloging-in-Publication Data

Tait, Leia.
  Queen Rania Al-Abdullah / Leia Tait.
    p. cm. -- (Remarkable people)
  Includes index.
  ISBN 978-1-59036-645-5 (hard cover : alk. paper) -- ISBN 978-1-59036-646-2 (soft
cover : alk. paper)
  1. Rania, Queen, consort of Abdullah II, King of Jordan, 1970---Juvenile literature.
2. Jordan--Kings and rulers--Biography--Juvenile literature. I. Title.
  DS154.52.R36T35 2007
  956.9504'4092--dc22
  [B]

                          2006036970

Printed in the United States of America
1 2 3 4 5 6 7 8 9 0 11 10 09 08 07

Editor: Leia Tait
Design: Terry Paulhus

Cover: Queen Rania is helping women and children around the world achieve their
goals and improve their lives.

Photograph Credits
Used with permission from Nabil Barto, Ambassador of the Hashemite Kingdom of
Jordan: page 7 top left.

Every reasonable effort has been made to trace ownership and to obtain
permission to reprint copyright material. The publishers would be pleased
to have any errors or omissions brought to their attention so that they may
be corrected in subsequent printings.

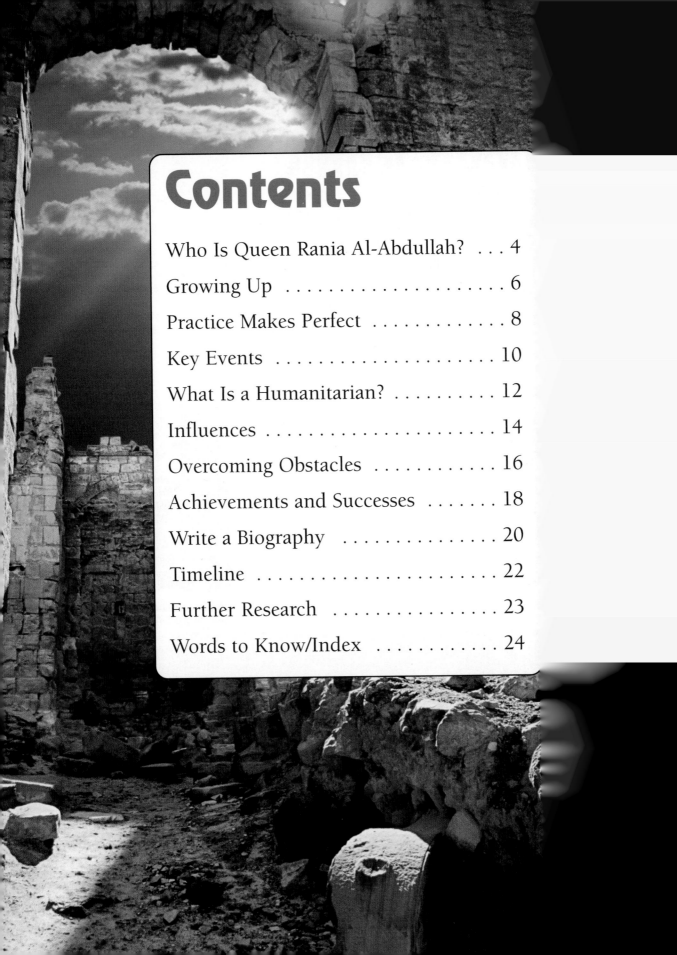

Contents

Who Is Queen Rania Al-Abdullah?

Queen Rania Al-Abdullah is the queen of Jordan. Jordan is a small country in the **Middle East**. As well as being a queen, Rania is a **humanitarian**. She works to improve the lives of people in Jordan. She also does important work for women and children around the world. Rania wants to make sure that all people can go to school. She wants everyone to be able to receive medical care and **financial** help when needed. Rania travels the world to promote these issues. She is truly a **role model** for others.

> *"I believe that we now have a challenge, and an opportunity, to help millions around the world make their hopes real."*

Growing Up

Rania was born in Kuwait on August 31, 1970. Kuwait is a rich country on the shore of the **Persian Gulf**. Rania's parents were from a part of Jordan that is now the West Bank. They had moved to Kuwait in 1967. Her father was a doctor. Her mother stayed home to care for the family. Rania grew up with her older sister, Dina, and her younger brother, Majdi. As a young girl, she went to New English School in Kuwait City. There, Rania learned to speak both **Arabic** and English.

In 1987, Rania went to Cairo, Egypt, to study business. She attended a school called the American University in Cairo. While she was there, an army from Iraq took over Kuwait. The ruler of Iraq was Saddam Hussein. He wanted to control Kuwait's oil supplies. Leaders from other countries, including the United States, sent their armies to help Kuwait. This conflict became the **First Persian Gulf War**. During the war, Rania's parents fled Kuwait and went to Jordan. Rania stayed in Egypt to finish her schooling. In 1991, she joined her parents in the city of Amman.

■ Parts of Kuwait City were destroyed during the First Persian Gulf War. Since then, it has been rebuilt and is an important business center.

Get to Know Jordan

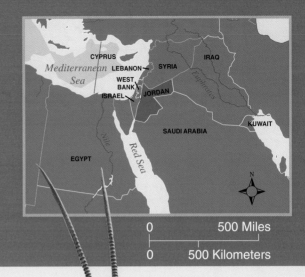

COAT OF ARMS

FLAG

FLOWER
Black Iris

0 — 500 Miles

0 — 500 Kilometers

Amman is the capital of Jordan. About 2 million people live there.

The Jordan River separates the country from Israel and the **West Bank**. It drains into the Dead Sea, the lowest point on Earth.

Some of the earliest settlements in history were on lands that are now part of Jordan.

The Arabian oryx is a type of rare antelope that lives in the deserts of Jordan.

Most Jordanians are Muslim. They follow the religion of **Islam**.

About 6 million people live in Jordan. Seventy percent of the population is younger than 30 years of age. What might be difficult about ruling such a young country? What might be some of the benefits?

Practice Makes Perfect

In Amman, Rania worked briefly in banking and then at a computer company. One evening in January 1993, her life changed. At a dinner party, Rania met Prince Abdullah bin Al-Hussein. Abdullah was the son of Jordan's King Hussein bin Al-Talal. Rania and Abdullah fell in love. They married on June 10, 1993.

In her new role as princess, Rania worked to improve the lives of Jordanians. In 1995, she founded the Jordan River Foundation (JRF). JRF helps women gain job skills and start small businesses. Rania founded the Child Safety Program in 1998. The program protects and counsels abused children in Jordan. It was the first program to help child abuse victims in the Middle East.

■ Jordanians lined the streets and cheered as Rania and Abdullah traveled to and from their wedding ceremony in 1993.

Rania's husband was a prince, but he did not expect to be king. His uncle was **heir** to the throne. However, in January 1999, King Hussein named Abdullah the new heir. Everyone was surprised. Later that year, Hussein passed away. Abdullah and Rania became king and queen of Jordan.

QUICK FACTS

- When Rania was crowned in 1999, she became the world's youngest living queen.
- Queen Rania has four children. Their names are Hussein, Iman, Salma, and Hashem.
- As queen of Jordan, Rania focuses her efforts on five key areas. They are education, health and safety, youth issues, women's rights, and culture and tourism.

As queen, Rania worked even harder. She continued to try to improve life for people in Jordan. She also traveled more. On her travels, Rania learned that women and children around the world face the same problems as Jordanians. She thought of ways that she could help all women and children. Rania shared her ideas with other powerful people.

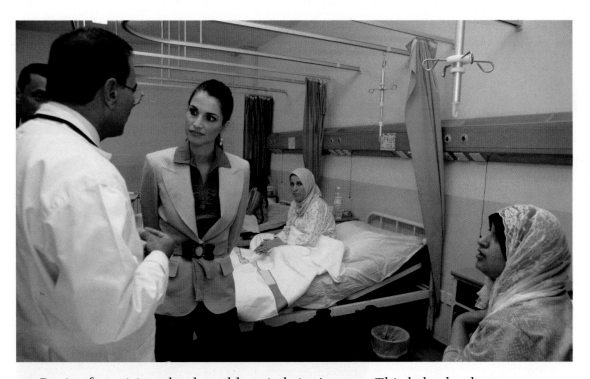

■ Rania often visits schools and hospitals in Amman. This helps her better understand the needs of Jordanians.

Key Events

As queen of Jordan, Rania has worked with many humanitarian groups. In 2000, she led the **Royal Commission** on Human Rights in Jordan. The commission made a plan to protect human rights for all Jordanians. That same year, Queen Rania began to help the **United Nations** Children's Fund (UNICEF) raise money for children's programs. She also organized aid for earthquake survivors in India, Iran, and Pakistan. In 2002, Rania joined the World **Economic** Forum (WEF). This group of world leaders helps improve living conditions around the world.

Rania has been featured in many magazines, including *People* and *Time*. She has appeared on television programs such as *BBC World, CNN Connects, Good Morning America,* and the *Oprah Winfrey Show.* Through her work, Rania has met many other important people, including Nelson Mandela, Oprah Winfrey, and Bill and Hillary Clinton.

■ In 2005, U.S. First Lady Laura Bush visited Queen Rania in Jordan.

Thoughts from Rania

Queen Rania often talks about human rights issues around the world. Here are some of her thoughts about her work.

Rania shares what she would like others to know about the Middle East.

"I do not want people to see only negative images, which too often fill the television screens. Rather, I want them to see in Jordan a land rich in culture, full of potential and populated by peace-loving citizens."

Rania believes young people are important.

"[Youth] are 100 percent of our future."

Rania promotes cooperation and understanding.

"Once you feel that others are like you, then you want for others what you want for yourself. And that way you start helping others."

Rania is an example for other women.

"The best advertisement for **empowering** women is an empowered woman."

Rania explains how becoming a mother influenced her humanitarian goals.

"If there is anything that motherhood has taught me, it is that I am not just a mother to my own children, but to every child that I encounter."

Rania explains why helping others is important to her.

"When you solve somebody else's problem, you're solving a problem for yourself because our world today is so interconnected."

What Is a Humanitarian?

Humanitarians are people who work to improve the lives of others. Some work to protect human rights for all people. Others focus on the rights of certain groups. They might focus on the rights of women, children, or those living in poverty.

Some humanitarians raise money for programs that make the world a better place. They take part in action groups. They write letters, speak to reporters, attend important events, and make public speeches. Well-known humanitarians, such as Queen Rania, urge others to help.

Some people earn a living through their humanitarian work. Others work for humanitarian causes in their free time, for no pay. Humanitarians come from all backgrounds, all parts of the world, and all age groups. Some are well known all around the world. Others are known only in their own communities. All of them help make important changes in society.

■ Rania enjoys connecting with the children and other people she meets through her work.

Humanitarians 101

Craig Kielburger (1982–)

Cause: Children's Rights
Achievements: Craig Kielburger works to end child labor around the world. In 1995, when he was just 12 years old, Kielburger started Free The Children (FTC). FTC promotes children's rights around the world. It is run by young people who want to help other young people. More than one million youths have been involved in FTC programs in more than 45 countries. In 2006, Kielburger received the World's Children's Prize for the Rights of the Child for his work with FTC.

Melinda Gates (1964–)

Cause: Medical Care, Education
Achievements: Melinda Gates is the co-founder and director of the Bill and Melinda Gates Foundation. The Gates Foundation gives money to help scientists discover cures for the world's deadliest diseases. Gates also works to improve education in the United States. The Gates Foundation funds programs that bring education to children in need. Through the foundation, Melinda and her husband, Bill, have donated more money to charity than anyone else in history.

Blessed Mother Teresa (1910–1997)

Cause: Medical Care, Poverty
Achievements: Blessed Mother Teresa was a nun. She spent her life caring for the poor and the sick in India. In 1948, she founded a **religious order** for women called the Order of the Missionaries of Charity. The order built medical centers to care for people who were blind, very old, disabled, or dying. In 1979, Blessed Mother Teresa received the Nobel Peace Prize. The Order of the Missionaries of Charity now runs hundreds of centers in more than 90 countries. Many people are working to have Blessed Mother Teresa declared a **saint**.

The 14th Dalai Lama (1935–)

Cause: Peace
Achievements: The 14th Dalai Lama is the religious and political leader of Tibet. In 1950, China invaded Tibet and took control of the country. The Dalai Lama tried to make peace with China. He did not succeed. In 1959, the Chinese army killed more than 80,000 Tibetans who tried to take back the country. The Dalai Lama fled to India. Since then, he has traveled to many countries to speak out against China's actions in Tibet. He promotes peace, tolerance, and freedom for all people. The Dalai Lama works with students, world leaders, and other humanitarians to further human rights. He was awarded the Nobel Peace Prize in 1989.

R PEDIATRIC & FAMILY MEDICAL CENTER is grateful for funding toward the Pharmacy

Henry L. Guenther Foundation

Foundations

Foundations are organizations created to benefit others. Most foundations focus on a certain cause, such as education or health care. Foundations begin with donations from individuals, groups, or governments. This money is used to support the foundation's cause. Some foundations give money to help young people go to school. Others fund medical research. Humanitarians create foundations for many different purposes.

Influences

The major influence in Rania's life is her family. Her husband is one of her role models. Abdullah's vision for Jordan inspires Rania's own work. They both want to improve life for people in Jordan and in other countries as well. When they face challenges in their work, Rania and Abdullah seek one another's advice. They energize and help each other.

Rania's children help her focus on what is most important to her—family. Rania often takes her children with her when she travels. She helps them with their homework and reads with them each night.

■ Even though she is very busy, Rania makes time for her family. They enjoy cooking, listening to music, and watching television together.

Having children has made Rania more aware of other young people. She urges people to listen to what children have to say about the world. While in Amman, Rania often visits schools and nearby towns to talk with youth. She enjoys listening to their ideas. "Every time I speak to our young people in Jordan, I am always inspired and I am always energized," she says. Rania's interest in youth around the world inspired her to join the International Youth Foundation in 2002.

Rania is often inspired by other women. She speaks with mothers, teachers, and farmers. She believes that women are changing the world. They are challenging traditional roles. They are gaining confidence. Rania has said that these women can make lasting changes by being role models for their children.

INTERNATIONAL YOUTH FOUNDATION (IYF)

The International Youth Foundation (IYF) was founded in 1990 by humanitarian Rick Little. IYF aims to create opportunities for children in need. The foundation helps young people access education, job training, life skills, and other opportunities for success. IYF works to increase global awareness of children and child welfare issues. Since it began, IYF has helped 26 million young people in more than 70 countries. To learn more about IYF, visit their website at **www.iyfnet.org**.

■ Rania is on the Board of Directors of IYF. In 2004, she visited with children at an IYF event in Ireland.

Overcoming Obstacles

Jordan is a country with ancient values and beliefs. Before Rania became queen, few Arab women took part in political life. Instead, women stayed home, caring for their husbands and children. Rania is different. She is an equal partner with her husband. Rania helps Abdullah carry out his work as Jordan's ruler. She looks after areas he does not have much time for. She gives him advice. Rania also pursues her own interests and leads important groups. She speaks out on topics, such as women's rights and child abuse, that were once forbidden to talk about.

Some people in Jordan and other Arab countries feel that Rania should not meddle in the king's affairs. They complain that her actions weaken family values. Others see Rania as a role model. They believe that her achievements prove that Arab women are smart and capable.

■ In some Muslim countries, women must cover their heads with veils. In Jordan, women can choose to wear a veil or not. Rania chooses not to wear one.

Rania faces many other challenges. War and **terrorism** are problems in the Middle East. Terrorists have bombed Jordan many times in the past. Attacks on other parts of the world have made many people afraid of the Middle East. Rania is upset by this. She wants to promote understanding between the Middle East and the rest of the world, especially the United States. Rania believes that people can stop terrorism by learning more about other cultures. She travels outside Jordan to share her culture with leaders, media, and students in other countries. Queen Rania and her country often act as a bridge between the Middle East and the rest of the world.

■ In 2003, King Abdullah and Queen Rania visited Washington, DC, to share their knowledge of the Middle East with U.S. politicians.

Achievements and Successes

Since becoming queen, Rania has helped countless people in many countries. She works with 15 international groups, including UNICEF, the WEF, the IYF, and the Foundation for International Community Assistance (FINCA). FINCA provides banking services to people living in poverty, so that they can create jobs and improve their lives.

In 2006, Rania joined the Board of Directors of the United Nations Foundation. The UN Foundation was founded in 1998 to strengthen and support the activities of the United Nations. Since 1998, the foundation has provided more than $900 million to UN projects in at least 115 countries.

■ In 2001, Rania received a Life Achievement Award from the Italian Government. The award recognized Rania's efforts in women's health.

Through her Jordan River Foundation, Rania has helped improve living conditions for women in Jordan and around the world. Jordanian women are now attending university in greater numbers than ever before. They are becoming involved in politics. More women are joining the Jordanian army, the police force, and the business world.

Many groups from around the world have recognized Rania's work. *Forbes Magazine* has ranked her among the 100 most powerful women in the world. In 2005, Rania became the first person to receive the Woman of the World Award from Women for Women International. Rania serves as the group's global **ambassador**. In 2006, Rania was recognized again. That year, the Queen Rania Family and Child Center, which is part of the Jordan River Foundation, received the 2006 Prevention of Child Abuse Prize from the Women's World Summit Foundation.

WOMEN FOR WOMEN INTERNATIONAL

Women for Women International was founded in 1993. The organization helps women around the world who have been affected by war. It provides counseling, financial support, education, and job training to help women rebuild their lives after war. Since 1993, Women for Women International has helped more than 73,000 women in countries such as Bosnia, Iraq, Nigeria, and Sudan. To learn more about Women for Women International, visit their website at **www.womenforwomen.org**.

Write a Biography

A person's life story can be the subject of a book. This kind of book is called a biography. Biographies describe the lives of remarkable people, such as those who have achieved great success or have done important things to help others. These people may be alive today or they may have lived many years ago. Reading a biography can help you learn more about a remarkable person.

At school, you might be asked to write a biography. First, decide who you want to write about. You can choose a humanitarian, such as Queen Rania, or any other person you find interesting. Then, find out if your library has any books about this person. Learn as much as you can about him or her. Write down the key events in this person's life. What was this person's childhood like? What has he or she accomplished? What are his or her goals? What makes this person special or unusual?

A concept web is a useful research tool. Read the questions in the following concept web. Answer the questions in your notebook. Your answers will help you write your biography.

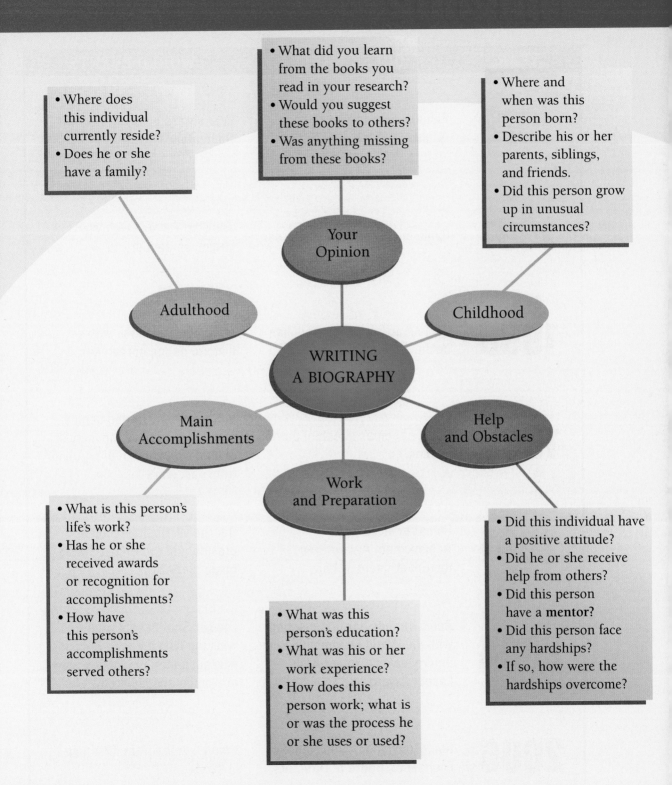

- Where does this individual currently reside?
- Does he or she have a family?

- What did you learn from the books you read in your research?
- Would you suggest these books to others?
- Was anything missing from these books?

- Where and when was this person born?
- Describe his or her parents, siblings, and friends.
- Did this person grow up in unusual circumstances?

Your Opinion

Adulthood

Childhood

WRITING A BIOGRAPHY

Main Accomplishments

Help and Obstacles

Work and Preparation

- What is this person's life's work?
- Has he or she received awards or recognition for accomplishments?
- How have this person's accomplishments served others?

- What was this person's education?
- What was his or her work experience?
- How does this person work; what is or was the process he or she uses or used?

- Did this individual have a positive attitude?
- Did he or she receive help from others?
- Did this person have a **mentor?**
- Did this person face any hardships?
- If so, how were the hardships overcome?

Timeline

YEAR	QUEEN RANIA	WORLD EVENTS
1970	Rania is born in Kuwait on August 31.	War breaks out in Jordan on September 17.
1991	Rania moves to Amman, Jordan.	The First Persian Gulf War begins on January 16.
1993	Rania marries Prince Abdullah on June 10.	Israel and Palestine sign a historic peace agreement.
1999	Rania becomes queen of Jordan in June.	In September, Jordan begins working to remove thousands of land mines left in the ground from past wars.
2001	Rania receives a Life Achievement Award from the Government of Italy.	George W. Bush becomes president of the United States on January 20.
2003	Rania attends her first meeting with the World Economic Forum and receives a Young Arab Leader Award.	Lawyer Shirin Ebadi from Iran wins the Nobel Peace Prize for her humanitarian work on behalf of women and children.
2006	Rania joins the United Nations Foundation Board of Directors.	Women vote for the first time in Kuwait.

Further Research

How can I find out more about Queen Rania Al-Abdullah?

Most libraries have computers that connect to a database for searching for information. If you input a key word, you will be provided with a list of books in the library that contain information on that topic. Non-fiction books are arranged numerically, using their call number. Fiction books are organized alphabetically by the author's last name.

Websites

To learn more about Queen Rania, visit
www.queenrania.jo

To learn more about Jordan, visit
www.visitjordan.com

Words to Know

ambassador: an official representative

Arabic: a language spoken in the Middle East

economic: relating to money systems

empowering: giving someone authority or confidence

financial: having to do with money

First Persian Gulf War: a conflict between Iraq and other countries that took place in early 1991

heir: the person next in line to be king or queen

humanitarian: somebody who tries to improve the lives of others

Islam: the religion based on the teachings of the prophet Muhammad

mentor: a wise and trusted teacher

Middle East: the area that includes Egypt, Israel, Jordan, Lebanon, Sudan, Syria, Turkey, Iraq, and Iran

Persian Gulf: a large body of water off the Arabian Sea

religious order: a group of religious people who follow the same way of life

role model: a person who others look up to

royal commission: a special group set up by the king to examine a certain issue

saint: someone who is recognized for leading a holy life dedicated to helping others

terrorism: the use of terror, often created through violence, to achieve a goal

United Nations: an organization made up of many countries of the world

West Bank: an area west of the Jordan River that was once part of Jordan but has been occupied by Israel since 1967

Index